$1
1/18
RKS

Bible Readers Series

A Study of Hebrews

Looking Forward in Faith

William J. Carter

AF811095

Abingdon Press / Nashville

LOOKING FORWARD IN FAITH
A STUDY OF HEBREWS

Copyright © 1987 by Cokesbury.
Revised Edition Copyright © 2001 by Abingdon Press.

All rights reserved.
No part of this work may be reproduced or transmitted in any form or by any means, electronic or mechanical, including photocopying and recording, or by any information storage or retrieval system, except as may be expressly permitted by the 1976 Copyright Act or in writing from the publisher. Requests for permission should be addressed in writing to Permissions Office, 201 Eighth Avenue, South, P.O. Box 801, Nashville, Tennessee 37202-0801, or faxed to 615-749-6512.

Scripture quotations in this publication, unless otherwise indicated, are from the New Revised Standard Version of the Bible, copyrighted © 1989 by the Division of Christian Education of the National Council of the Churches of Christ in the United States of America, and are used by permission.

Lessons are based on the International Sunday School Lessons for Christian Teaching, copyright © 1984, by the Committee on the Uniform Series.

This book is printed on acid-free paper.

ISBN 0-687-09515-8

01 02 03 04 05 06 07 08 09 10—10 9 8 7 6 5 4 3 2 1
Manufactured in the United States of America.

CONTENTS

Chapter One

God's Living Word

PURPOSE

To recognize the supreme importance for our salvation of God's self-revelation in the person of Jesus

BIBLE PASSAGE

Hebrews 1:1-5

1 **Long ago God spoke to our ancestors in many and var-
ious ways by the prophets,** 2 **but in these last days he has
spoken to us by a Son, whom he appointed heir of all things,
through whom he also created the worlds.** 3 **He is the
reflection of God's glory and the exact imprint of God's
very being, and he sustains all things by his powerful word.
When he had made purification for sins, he sat down at the
right hand of the Majesty on high,** 4 **having become as
much superior to angels as the name he has inherited is
more excellent than theirs.**

5 **For to which of the angels did God ever say,**

> **"You are my Son;**
> **today I have begotten you"?**
>
> **Or again,**
>
> **"I will be his Father,**
> **and he will be my Son"?**

Hebrews 2:1-5, 9-10

1 **Therefore we must pay greater attention to what we**
have heard, so that we do not drift away from it. 2 **For if**
the message declared through angels was valid, and every
transgression or disobedience received a just penalty,
3 **how can we escape if we neglect so great a salvation? It**
was declared at first through the Lord, and it was attested to
us by those who heard him, 4 **while God added his testi-**
mony by signs and wonders and various miracles, and by
gifts of the Holy Spirit, distributed according to his will.
5 **Now God did not subject the coming world, about**
which we are speaking, to angels. . . .
9 **But we do see Jesus, who for a little while was made**
lower than the angels, now crowned with glory and honor
because of the suffering of death, so that by the grace of
God he might taste death for everyone.
10 **It was fitting that God, for whom and through whom all**
things exist, in bringing many children to glory, should make
the pioneer of their salvation perfect through sufferings.

CORE VERSES

Long ago God spoke to our ancestors in many and various ways by the prophets, but in these last days he has spoken to us by a Son. (Hebrews 1:1-2)

OUR NEED

The line between arrogance and personal assurance in the Christian faith is narrow. We want to recognize God's unending provision for our lives and to give appropriate credit for all good things, but we also need to recognize that it is possible to claim more of God's favor than we deserve. Because we are rich in the goods of the world or blessed with good health or filled with joy does not mean that we can assume that God is approving all that we do. To do so would be spiritual arrogance.

Some of the greatest Christians of all time never received visible rewards for their labors but left enduring legacies, while others who had every sign of success in the field of religion left only hollow spaces when they departed. The good life is its own reward and does not need to display external proof. A bad life is not made better by the achievement of fame and fortune.

The following chapters will deal with the theme "Looking Forward in Faith." We will be looking at both what God *provides* for us and what God *requires* of us. In that process we may begin to see some ways we can distinguish between genuine thanksgiving for God's grace and care and claiming favoritism that is not rightfully ours.

We begin with "God's Living Word," which will remind us of the importance of serving the Lord who became the Word of God made flesh.

FAITHFUL LIVING

As a result of contact with other religions in the area, some of the people of the Jewish faith had become fascinated with the concept of angels. While angels are mentioned in the Old Testament, the Hebrews had never allowed the worship of angels to intrude on the worship of the one true God. Now many people were beginning to consider angels only a little lower than God and to include them in worship practices. Perhaps that is why the writer of Hebrews made such a point of comparing Jesus to the angels. Since the letter was written for the common people, many of whom felt that angels were superior beings, it seemed appropriate to show just how important Jesus was by pointing out that he was superior to angels.

While most Christians today accept the description of Jesus as fully human and fully divine, that certainly was not the case in the first century. Each new group had to be convinced, especially the Hebrews who had always believed that God was not to be represented in human form.

In order to address that question, the writer of Hebrews pointed out that Jesus "for a little while was made lower than the angels" (Hebrews 2:9). To put it another way: Jesus was made human. Many of the people had experienced Jesus as a human being, but others had not. It was important for all of them to understand that God had been in the midst of them in a form like their own. The humanity of Jesus was important because only in the Word made flesh could God's saving power be brought to created beings.

The point of the writing was to magnify the risen Christ. Even if he had once been one with humanity, he is now "much superior to angels" (Hebrews 1:4). Angels have no real control over the world and are not to be seen as even remotely like Jesus Christ. Hebrews 1:6 says, "Let all God's angels worship him." Only Jesus Christ is the "heir of all things" (1:2). Only through Jesus Christ does salvation come. God has provided the perfect way for those who will seek to come to him: a Savior who is fully human and fully divine.

In what ways did Jesus show he was human, and in what ways did he show his divinity while he was on earth?

The Plan of Salvation

The writer of Hebrews warns us not to "neglect so great a salvation" (2:3). What follows is a review of the way Scripture reveals that plan of salvation.

- The ***preparation phase*** in which God demonstrated the futility of attempting to gain salvation by the performance of religious acts and ceremonies lasted throughout the entire period of time before the birth of Jesus. The Old Testament is filled with references to the gradual awakening of Israel to the idea that God desires righteousness and not sacrifice. The final stage in this phase is the preparation, through the prophets, for the recognition of the Savior.

- The ***Incarnation,*** when the Word was made flesh and dwelt among human beings, was an essential step. God was in Christ, Paul said, reconciling the world unto himself. It is this aspect that makes possible the remainder. In order to redeem an errant world, God became part of it, participating in its activities and enduring its suffering. Born into the same situation that others are born into, he made himself one with humanity in order to bridge the gap between the human and the divine.
- The ***Crucifixion*** became the focal point of the entire cosmos when Jesus endured the final human experience in order to take upon himself the sins of the whole world. Perfect unity exists at that point. Paul said in Colossians 1:15-20, "He is the image of the invisible God, the firstborn of all creation; . . . all things have been created through him and for him. He himself is before all things, and in him all things hold together. He is the head of the body, the church; he is the beginning, the firstborn from the dead, so that he might come to have first place in everything. For in him all the fullness of God was pleased to dwell, and through him God was pleased to reconcile to himself all things, whether on earth or in heaven, by making peace through the blood of his cross." Jesus' death on the cross was the center of the plan of salvation.
- The ***Resurrection*** was the completion. Without it the rest would have been unbelievable. With it the whole process was made clear. He who could conquer death was able to conquer sin as well. "If you confess with your lips that Jesus is Lord and believe in your heart that God raised him from the dead, you will be saved" (Romans 10:9).
- The ***Holy Spirit*** confirmed the presence of God in the heart of persons. The Spirit, given to provide a continuing

evidence of God's ongoing love, also became the source of gifts through which persons were able to serve the God who had redeemed them. These gifts, many of them quite ordinary on the surface, were the means by which the whole body, the church, could be built up and made to serve the Creator.

- Finally, the plan of salvation included the ***church.*** In the passage above from Colossians 1, it is clear that the church is not an accident. It is clearly a major ingredient in the plan itself. The role of the church is stated clearly in the Letter to the Ephesians: "to make everyone see what is the plan . . . that *through the church* the wisdom of God in its rich variety might now be made known to the rulers and authorities in the heavenly places" (3:9-10, italics mine). The church is to inform heaven! It must not be despised but magnified. Those who claim to be in ministry outside its bounds must prove themselves by rigid standards, for it is through the church that God speaks to the world and beyond.

Those who try to distill the plan of salvation into a set of catchy phrases are doomed to failure. While they may capture some of it sometimes, they will never be able to express it all unless and until they include all these elements in their final statement. "In Christ God was reconciling the world to himself . . . and entrusting the message of reconciliation to us" (2 Corinthians 5:19).

What part of God's plan for salvation most affected your decision for Christ?

The Living Word

The Christian faith is based on a series of experiences that bring the Word to life. Let us review some of those experiences.

- ***The Word became alive in Creation.*** The Old Testament begins with a poetic recounting of the process of bringing the universe into being. I have no doubt that it describes the process through which it all happened. The account in Genesis agrees remarkably with what the scientific community has discovered about the Creation sequence. But the point of Creation is not the physical events, it is the way in which God invested himself in what he had made. Instead of leaving Creation to its own devices, God worked with and within it to make it his own. God's Word was alive in the Creation; in his relationship with the chosen people, Israel; and among all nations.

- ***The Word came alive in the person of Jesus Christ.*** The Gospel of John also opens with a poetic statement, this time about the relationship between the eternal Word and the Word made flesh. As the Genesis statement relates God to the created world, the statement in John relates God to all of humanity. "The Word became flesh and lived among us" (1:14). God was not only in the heavens, he was also among the people of earth.

It was not an accident that Jesus was fully human. Look at this passage of Scripture: "Christ Jesus,

> who, though he was in the form of God,
>   did not regard equality with God
>   as something to be exploited,
> but emptied himself,
>   taking the form of a slave,
>   being born in human likeness."
>
> (Philippians 2:5-7)

It was part of God's plan from the beginning to be subject to all the limits of human existence. Only in that way could God demonstrate how much he loved us and how we might learn to bear those limits ourselves. God's living Word not only saves us from sin, it saves us from our tendency to feel that being human is an unbearable disability.

- ***The Word is alive in Scripture.*** The Bible is a collection of the most remarkable religious documents ever recorded.

They are so varied and so vivid in their portrayal of the lives of people of faith and the ways they related to God and to one another that they are excellent sources for literary works. Thousands of novels, films, and musical compositions have been based on them. Yet, this same material contains the communication of God to his people in ways that enable them to learn about him, to discover his salvation, and to become his disciples. The Bible is truly the Word of God. It is a living Word that never becomes outdated or irrelevant. As surely as Jesus lived on earth, he continues to live in Scripture, along with all the other acts of God that are necessary for our fulfillment as human beings.

- Finally, ***God's Word is alive in the heart of his people.*** When persons accept Christ and become new creatures, they also gain new life. Paul said, "It is no longer I who live, but it is Christ who lives in me. And the life I now live in the flesh I live by faith in the Son of God" (Galatians 2:20).

This new aliveness is shown in a number of ways. The behavior of persons changes. They become more loving, responsive, and just. But, most of all, the presence and power of God shows itself in every part of life. Through the Holy Spirit the continuity of God among us is maintained and the Comforter that was promised keeps the Word alive in our heart.

The Word is brought to life each time a disciple applies it to the environment. It is the living Word when it is shared with others who need to know Christ as their Savior. It is enlivened when stirring music is sung in the worship service. It is made alive when it becomes the source of efforts to increase equality and justice among the nations and races. It comes to life in all situations where Christian people challenge the conventional wisdom of the world and seek to reflect the wisdom of the Prince of Peace. So long as a Christian is left on earth, the Word will always be alive.

When are you most alive in Christ? How does it make you feel?

So Great a Salvation

The challenge of this chapter is to rediscover the joy of salvation. Reviewing the plan of God and remembering the coming of Jesus Christ help us recognize the supreme importance of that event for our salvation. We have no other way to find a cure for our sin or a resource for living. God's living Word brings us to life in Christ.

CLOSING PRAYER

Creator and Redeemer, the One who has made us as we are, we pray that you will make us as we ought to be so that we may rejoice with you in the salvation of the world. Through Jesus Christ we pray. Amen.

2

Chapter Two

GOD'S PROMISE OF REST

PURPOSE

To understand the relationship between obedience to God and living confidently in the midst of daily stress and anxiety

BIBLE PASSAGE

Hebrews 3:12-19

12 **Take care, brothers and sisters, that none of you may have**
an evil, unbelieving heart that turns away from the living God.
13 **But exhort one another every day, as long as it is called**
"today," so that none of you may be hardened by the deceitful-
ness of sin. 14 **For we have become partners of Christ, if only**
we hold our first confidence firm to the end. 15 **As it is said,**

> **"Today, if you hear his voice,**
> **do not harden your hearts as in the**
> **rebellion."**

16 **Now who were they who heard and yet were rebellious?**
Was it not all those who left Egypt under the leadership of
Moses? 17 **But with whom was he angry forty years? Was it**
not those who sinned, whose bodies fell in the wilderness?
18 **And to whom did he swear that they would not enter his**
rest, if not to those who were disobedient? 19 **So we see**
that they were unable to enter because of unbelief.

Hebrews 4:1-2, 9-13
1 Therefore, while the promise of entering his rest is still open, let us take care that none of you should seem to have failed to reach it. 2 For indeed the good news came to us just as to them; but the message they heard did not benefit them, because they were not united by faith with those who listened. . . .
9 So then, a sabbath rest still remains for the people of God; 10 for those who enter God's rest also cease from their labors as God did from his. 11 Let us therefore make every effort to enter that rest, so that no one may fall through such disobedience as theirs.
12 Indeed, the word of God is living and active, sharper than any two-edged sword, piercing until it divides soul from spirit, joints from marrow; it is able to judge the thoughts and intentions of the heart. 13 And before him no creature is hidden, but all are naked and laid bare to the eyes of the one to whom we must render an account.

CORE VERSE

We have become partners of Christ, if only we hold our first confidence firm to the end. (Hebrews 3:14)

OUR NEED

During the last few years we have heard a great deal of talk about stress, which is said to lead to anxiety and eventually to "burn-out." In its simplest form, stress is not necessarily due to hard work or heavy responsibilities but results from our response to any part of life that makes us feel inadequate or threatened. Authors have written many books on the subject, and psychologists and counselors have given much advice on it.

Of course, stress is a factor in human health. We have

known for a long time that many illnesses are psychosomatic, which means that they are caused by something mental rather than by something physical. Stress also is a factor in spiritual health because feelings of guilt and failure can be a great detriment to confident spiritual living. In addition, people are different by their very nature; and some people suffer more stress than others even when they have the same experiences.

Whatever the causes or results of stress, Christians have ways to cope with it. Among the resources God provides is the promised rest and comfort described in our Bible Passage.

FAITHFUL LIVING

For people who had grown up in the Hebrew faith, no other event was as important as the Exodus. The escape from Egypt, the wandering in the wilderness, and the conquest of Canaan became the foundation stones of the faith of the nation of Israel. Many religious celebrations helped the people remember these events; and they constantly referred to these experiences in songs, writings, and conversation.

Since the early Jewish Christians were part of that tradition, they also made references to the experiences of the Exodus. The writer of the Letter to the Hebrews thus uses the framework of the Exodus to explain the meaning of faith. In the verses in our Bible Passage, he makes special mention of the rebellious group who fought against the leadership of Moses, built a golden calf, and finally died in the wilderness. God determined, he says, that "they shall not enter my rest" (Hebrews 4:5). The reason is obvious: They could not enter God's rest because they were not obedient to God's will.

Rebellious people cannot enter the rest that God has

promised. Only persons who keep the faith to the end are eligible. "For we have become partners of Christ, if only we hold our first confidence firm to the end" (Hebrews 3:14). The early Christians found that full participation in the benefits of the reign of God depended on a willingness to give full obedience to what God required.

God's promise of rest, then, is not offered without cost. The price is "faith with those who listened" (4:2). Those who believe and persevere will find rest. Those who rebel against God may not hope for rest as long as their rebellion continues.

What are some ways that rebellion robs us of peace of mind?

What Is the Promised Rest?

Two interpretations of the rest that was promised to the faithful are possible. One of these interpretations comes from the experience of entering the promised land of Canaan, when the people of the Exodus were able to put down their arms and rest from battle. The other comes from the rest that God gave himself after Creation. It is not always easy to tell which interpretation these verses are talking about. The third chapter of Hebrews (verses 16-19) clearly cites the Exodus experience; but the fourth chapter (verses 1-11) specifically refers to the rest that God took after creating the world, with the recommendation that we seek to enter that sabbath rest ourselves.

As is often true in the Bible, we must be able to join together these ideas in order to understand what is being said. Neither the wilderness nor the Creation describes the precise rest that is meant. We should understand this rest as a wider concept that includes both. It is a sabbath rest, but it is one that draws us from concern with the wilderness of daily living into a steady vision of the eternal life in Jesus Christ. It is not a rest that relieves us of responsibility or ends our journey, but it is one that provides us with the possibility of viewing all creation in such a way as to make it possible to live with serenity and confidence. This rest is available to all who accept Jesus Christ and who are obedient to the call of God. Unrest comes from the divided loyalties of a disordered life. Rest is the condition that surrounds us when all things are properly in focus. God's rest is a richer heritage than the milk and honey of the Promised Land. It is the calm of the soul that follows true faith.

The rest God promises us may not be rest at all if we understand it to be the absence of work. In Hebrews 4:10, we learn that "those who enter God's rest also cease from their labors as God did from his." But the catch is that God has never finally ceased from his labors. Throughout history God has continued to struggle with creation in order to bring it back to what he intended for it to be in the beginning. The key is the establishment of clear intentions. After God had finished the task of forming a world that could sustain itself, he could rest. Anything thereafter was part of his original intention. God no longer found it necessary to shake the foundations or to change the structure. All that was necessary was to bring what he intended to fulfillment, a task in which he is still involved.

We all know how we are completely overwhelmed at times by the demands that family, church, and community make on us. At other times the same demands make us feel appreciated and wanted. The difference is not in the demand, it is in the condition of the mind and heart.

In the same way, the rest promised to the Christian comes from the absence of contrary purposes and the presence of an inner unity that springs from our awareness of God in the totality of the new life in Christ.

When have you felt most at peace with yourself? Can you recall what caused you to feel that way?

Active Rest

We must enjoy the rest that is promised in the context of the Word of God. Clearly the Word is more than Scripture. It also is the indwelling of God in the whole of human experience. It is the Word in the sense of the first chapter of the Gospel of John. This Word is not restful; it is demanding. We know a number of things about it from the account in Hebrews 4:12.

The Word is "living and active." It must come alive in and for us. It never can be of the letter only; it must be constantly enlivened by the Spirit. The Spirit interprets the Word in us anew each day. The Word is either active in us or is not in us at all. The Word has power. God's rest is not withdrawal from the active life of faith but a more effective involvement in it.

The Word is "sharper than any two-edged sword." It cuts away superficial aspects and trims life down to the essentials. When we think of rest, we often imagine a time of leisure amid the trappings of luxury. The sharpness of the Word reminds us that the landscape of the faith holds no such vacation spots. We always have decisions to make, purposes to realize, and tasks to accomplish. These responsibilities bring joy instead of tension because they clearly are a part of the triumphant life in Jesus Christ.

The Word is "piercing until it divides soul from spirit, joints from marrow; it is able to judge the thoughts and intentions of the heart." It separates the created person (soul) from the redeemed person (spirit). We sometimes hide behind good intentions when our actions hurt other people; but the intentions of the heart reveal the true being of the person, rather than that person's declared motivations. We cannot rest in our own rationalizations. True rest comes only with full self-disclosure, when we acknowledge before God who we really are and what we are about. "Before him no creature is hidden, but all are naked and laid bare" (Hebrews 4:13).

We clearly see that identifying the promised rest with idleness or a sheltered life is not intended. The promised rest is, instead, a condition within which we can live life to the fullest. The restful aspects are internal, affecting the attitudes and meanings of our work rather than decreasing the work itself. The key to this internal security is obedience to the Word of God and faith in God's purpose for our life.

Is external or internal rest more helpful to you? Why?

Confident Living

If the rest promised by God is not a vacation from life's cares, then what is it? The answer to that question is the heart of our Bible Passage.

One way of seeing the value of a cure is to learn more about the effects of the illness. Just how does stress affect us, and what can God's promises do to help? One author has identified four symptoms of stress. Let us examine them and suggest ways that God's rest may help us counter them.

- One symptom is ***delayed decision making***. People who are suffering from too much stress are unable to make decisions in ordinary situations. All of us procrastinate, of course; and at times we are indecisive. But stress makes those situations much worse. How does the presence of God help us overcome that symptom?

The usual explanation for the inability to make small decisions is that we are worried about the larger decisions of life. When we are about to get married or divorced or change jobs or move to another part of the country, we tend to spend our internal energies on making those decisions. We find ourselves unable to decide which tie to wear with the brown suit or which sauce to put on the spaghetti. (I usually wind up with the spaghetti sauce on the tie!)

When the big decisions finally have been made, we find that the smaller ones fall into place. We either make those decisions with ease or find that they no longer matter.

One of the secrets of God's rest is that when we become obedient to God's will for our life, we have taken care of the biggest decision of all, which frees us to deal with the trivial without losing composure.

- Another symptom of stress is ***disorganization***. We cannot seem to "get it all together." While most of us have periods when we seem to run around in circles, the person suffering from stress is more likely to have those feelings most of the time. Often we are unable to focus clearly on our goals, and we have difficulty pointing our energies in any specific direction. Lacking any clear long-term goals, we wander from one thing to another with no connecting theme or purpose.

When we meet God's offer with faith (Hebrews 4:2), we find that life becomes more manageable. Purposes are clearer because the great purpose has been established. When we are living for Christ, and Christ only, the ultimate goal of our life is set. Other goals fall into place. While life never will be free of loose ends, it will be more focused and less apt to come apart. God's rest becomes our resource.

- ***Defensiveness*** is another symptom of stress. Because we feel unsure of ourselves, we often believe that other people are criticizing us unfairly or attacking us with no reason, even when they are just being friendly.

Someone has identified the cause of defensiveness as "authority anxiety," which means that since we are unsure of our own authority, we feel we must constantly defend it. When we give God the reins of our life, we settle the matter of authority forever. God is Lord. What we have is not our own but God's. Even our opinions are subject to God's Word. Humility becomes possible because we know that we are only stewards of all things, which come from God. God's rest makes us accepting and acceptable.

- The final symptom of stress is ***depression.*** When we can no longer cope with life, we withdraw within ourselves and become despondent. While much depression may be due to physical causes and need the care of a physician, at times depression springs from a sense of hopelessness and helplessness. Accepting God's offer of rest brings new life and meaning, dispelling the gloom of depression and restoring the spirit of hope.

A definite relationship exists between living for God through Christ and living with confidence and serenity. We will discover that obedience to God's will makes our life more joyous.

What are some ways in which you have experienced God's rest?

CLOSING PRAYER

O God, our redeemer, save us from ourselves through your power to lift us to yourself. In Christ's name we pray. Amen.

Chapter Three

God's Great High Priest

PURPOSE

To understand how the compassion of God in Christ offers a sure hope for our life

BIBLE PASSAGE

Hebrews 4:14-16

14 **Since, then, we have a great high priest who has**
passed through the heavens, Jesus, the Son of God, let us
hold fast to our confession. 15 **For we do not have a high**
priest who is unable to sympathize with our weaknesses, but
we have one who in every respect has been tested as we are,
yet without sin. 16 **Let us therefore approach the throne**
of grace with boldness, so that we may receive mercy and
find grace to help in time of need.

Hebrews 6:19-20

19 **We have this hope, a sure and steadfast anchor of the**
soul, a hope that enters the inner shrine behind the curtain,
20 **where Jesus, a forerunner on our behalf, has entered,**
having become a high priest forever according to the order
of Melchizedek.

Hebrews 7:21-28

21 **This one became a priest with an oath, because of the one who said to him,**

"The Lord has sworn
and will not change his mind,
'You are a priest forever.' "—

22 **accordingly Jesus has also become the guarantee of a better covenant.**

23 **Furthermore, the former priests were many in num-**
ber, because they were prevented by death from continuing
in office; 24 but he holds his priesthood permanently,
because he continues forever. 25 Consequently he is able
for all time to save those who approach God through him,
since he always lives to make intercession for them.

26 **For it was fitting that we should have such a high**
priest, holy, blameless, undefiled, separated from sinners,
and exalted above the heavens. 27 Unlike the other high
priests, he has no need to offer sacrifices day after day, first
for his own sins, and then for those of the people; this he
did once for all when he offered himself. 28 For the law
appoints as high priests those who are subject to weakness,
but the word of the oath, which came later than the law,
appoints a Son who has been made perfect forever.

CORE VERSE

Since, then, we have a great high priest who has passed through the heavens, Jesus, the Son of God, let us hold fast to our confession. (Hebrews 4:14)

OUR NEED

Christian leadership always has been difficult to define. Leadership takes so many forms in meeting so many needs that it has not been easy to develop descriptions of the varieties of service. In seminary I learned one way of describing the types of administration required of leaders. That description involved three modes of leading based on models from the Bible.

- Christian leaders sometimes need to be ***pastoral.*** The pastor is concerned about the welfare of each person and about the task of providing resources to enable persons to cope with daily life and to grow spiritually. Pastors are necessary because they give support to Christians as they develop discipleship.
- The ***prophetic*** function is needed also. Simply to comfort and support persons is not enough. They must also be reminded of the Lord's requirements and called upon to meet their responsibilities. The gospel is not always comforting. It demands sacrifice and witness as well as peace of mind.
- The ***priestly*** function also is important. Protestants have tended to think that the priestly function is not as valuable as the others. But someone must protect the integrity of the faith, provide the sacraments, and maintain tradition. The Christian faith has religious observances and ceremonies that witness to the power of God and maintain the authority of the church. We may have neglected the priestly function too much in our desire to elevate the prophetic and pastoral characteristics.

The Letter to the Hebrews witnesses to the value of the priestly function in a way unlike any other New Testament book. It reinterprets the priestly function to include an emphasis on compassion, the new dimension God's presence in Christ has given to the priesthood.

FAITHFUL LIVING

The priesthood had great importance for the people of Israel. Although they began with a general priesthood, in which each head of a household could offer sacrifices, they soon set aside the tribe of Levi for special services to the Tabernacle. It is not clear exactly what these persons did; but in the Exodus one of the members of the tribe, Aaron, was given full priestly duties that were maintained by his family throughout most of the history of Israel. Not only did these people have religious responsibilities, they also exercised power in the administration of the government and were involved in the anointing of kings.

When the prophets arose, the priests fell into disrepute. A number of charges were leveled against them, including living in luxury off the proceeds of the Temple (Amos 6:4-6), interpreting the laws so strictly that they became a hindrance instead of a help, turning from the worship of the true God (Hosea 4:4-6), and failing to stress righteousness while they asked for sacrifices (Micah 6:6-8). Not until the time of Ezra did the priesthood regain its former respectability. With the rebuilding of the Temple and the restoration of the nation after the Exile, the concept of priestly rule returned. During the years before the birth of Jesus, the high priests (such as Jonathan, Simon, and Hyrcanus II) were also the leaders of the army and the government.

The high priest and others of his group were instrumental in the trial and crucifixion of Jesus. No wonder the early Christians did not think highly of the priesthood and avoided any identification with it in their worship practices. But as descendants of Judaism, the early Christians still felt a need for the priestly function. The writer of Hebrews was able to find a way to give them the priesthood they desired in a form that was completely compatible with their experience of salvation. The presentation of Jesus as the new high priest, in the order of Melchizedek, helped them unite the old with the new and provided for generations of Christians a way to understand the relationship of Christ to the community of faith.

What priestly functions does your pastor perform? How are those functions important to your church? to you?

The New High Priest

The Bible contains no references to Jesus as high priest or any identification of Melchizedek in other parts of the New Testament, so we must depend on the Old Testament for our understanding. The writer of Hebrews draws from the story of Abraham's meeting with the king and priest of Salem for his comparison (Genesis 14:17-20). Salem was the old name of the place that later became Jerusalem. The actual phrase, "priest forever, / according to the order of Melchizedek" (Hebrews 7:17) is in Psalm 110:4.

From these sources Hebrews provides a description of the ways in which Jesus qualifies as high priest.

- ***He was "called."*** Priests must be called to service. Jesus was called at his baptism; but, more important, he was called from the beginning of the world. He had "passed through the heavens" (Hebrews 4:14).
- ***He was able to offer sacrifice.*** The sacrifice Jesus offered was himself, to be sure; but that only made the qualification the more valuable because, unlike the sacrifices of the priests in the Temple, this sacrifice never had to be repeated.
- ***He was sympathetic to the needs of his people.*** Every high priest should have this quality (Hebrews 5:1-2), but Jesus had it supremely. When Jesus became flesh and died on the cross, he suffered with and for his people. Compassion, which means to suffer with, was the result.

Unlike other high priests, Jesus will reign forever. He is alive forever, so his priesthood will never cease. In this respect Jesus is like Melchizedek, who was "without father, without mother, without genealogy, having neither beginning of days nor end of life" (Hebrews 7:3).

How are the priesthood of the Old Testament and the priesthood of Jesus alike? How are they different?

Covenant and Compassion

Priests traditionally gained office through heredity. The son replaced the father. Jesus, however, was appointed to the position because of the life he lived (Hebrews 7:16). The writer reminds us that various types of priesthood had succeeded one another (the Levites, Aaron, and so on), but the priesthood of Jesus would last forever.

"Jesus has also become the guarantee of a better covenant" (7:22). The new covenant is in the blood of Jesus Christ. Each time Holy Communion is served, it reminds its partakers that the new High Priest represents a new relationship between God and humanity. God's intention to establish this better covenant is guaranteed by the presence of Jesus Christ in the world (the "guarantee," Hebrews 7:22) and by his continued existence in the presence of God.

A major characteristic of this new relationship is grace, which is represented in the sympathy that Jesus has for our weaknesses (Hebrews 4:15) and implies a compassion far beyond that of the previous covenants or their high priests. Instead of a legalistic insistence on the letter of the law, the emphasis is on forgiveness and redemption.

The compassion of God in Jesus is important to us, and we will examine it in some detail during the remainder of this chapter.

What is your understanding of your agreement (covenant) with God? Are you satisfied with that agreement? Why or why not?

Compassion and Hope

A considerable difference exists between a system based on justice and one based on mercy. While we all admire the aims of justice and hope that we will have the benefits of a just society, we are aware that mercy is what we really need.

The nature of God as revealed through Jesus Christ is compassion. God loved us before we knew him. God longs for our redemption. God seeks to make us his own. God will not hold our sins against us. The cross is our guarantee of God's endless concern for us. This emphasis on mercy and compassion has a number of implications for us.

Compassion means that we can count on God to attempt to rescue us even when our predicaments are of our own making. God never tires of reconciliation. Most of the time the world adds to our misery instead of seeking our relief. When we are deeply in debt, the interest rates may go up; and when we have an accident, our insurance may be cancelled. But when we are in trouble, God is all the more determined to bring us back to new life. One of the greatest certainties we have is that "in all these things we are more than conquerors through him who loved us" (Romans 8:37). We can have a sure hope that God will continue to care for us at every station of life, even in the midst of our most sinful circumstances.

We are expected to show the same mercies. We are warned repeatedly not to judge others who seem to be in error. Romans 14:13 warns, "Let us therefore no longer pass judgment on one another, but resolve instead never to put a stumbling block or hindrance in the way of another." Christians have a history of sometimes vicious prejudices against people of other races, against persons who use other Scripture translations, against persons with alternative lifestyles, against different political systems from the one we happen to live in. God expects us to leave judgment to him and to base our own life on the compassion that God showed in the death of Jesus. Our Lord himself counseled that we should let the weeds grow with the wheat until the harvest. We can ensure our hope of God's compassion by practicing it ourselves.

Compassion also means that our life will always have meaning. Even if we seem to be living in obscure circumstances and doing only what is necessary to make life bearable for us and for fellow human beings, we still are participating in a priesthood so universal that every sparrow counts. No action is wasted. Even the smallest act of compassion performed on behalf of someone else is part of the whole realm of the mercy of God. We have a sure hope that our life will have significance, even if it does not have prominence.

Just as the former high priests were a pathway to God for the worshipers in the Temple, so Jesus as High Priest is the avenue of God's salvation to persons who will believe. The level of certainty is much greater, and the promise is richer and more lasting; but the process is the same. Through the offering of the sacrificial lamb (in this case, Jesus), the priest lifts to God the cause of the sinner and assures forgiveness and salvation. This hope is the greatest of all. It assures that life will not only be lived in its fullest measure but that life will have no end to it. "He is able for all time to save those who approach God through him" (Hebrews 7:25).

In what ways have you received compassion from God or from others? In what ways have you given compassion?

A Sure Hope in Christ

To our modern ears Hebrews' theme may seem less important than the Passion story or the letters of Paul or the great treatise on love in First John, but what we have to remember is that it takes all these aspects to make a full picture of who Jesus Christ is and what a Christian is expected to be. The whole gospel is found only in a consideration of all the Scripture. Partial gospels lead some people to practice a narrow faith. We need to look at the whole range of meanings that Jesus represented. Those persons who get caught up in theories of the Atonement or who concentrate on speaking in tongues or who are obsessed with the millennial controversies fail to view this whole range. The whole gospel represents salvation, not just one of its portions.

The concept of Jesus as High Priest adds to our understanding of the whole gospel of Jesus Christ. It helps us see that we are part of a continuing experience with a God who cares so much for us that he provides continuous self-revelations to ensure that we will be able to see through one or more of them a vision of this saving grace. The whole gospel contains a sure hope for our life and our salvation.

CLOSING PRAYER

God, the Creator of our life, enable us to live such lives of concern for others that we may reflect your concern for us. Through Jesus Christ, the High Priest and our Lord, we pray. Amen.

4

Chapter Four

God's New Covenant

PURPOSE

To learn how God's new covenant in Jesus Christ fulfills the old covenant

BIBLE PASSAGE

Hebrews 9:15-28

15 **For this reason he is the mediator of a new covenant,
so that those who are called may receive the promised eter-
nal inheritance, because a death has occurred that redeems
them from the transgressions under the first covenant.**
16 **Where a will is involved, the death of the one who made
it must be established.** 17 **For a will takes effect only at
death, since it is not in force as long as the one who made it
is alive.** 18 **Hence not even the first covenant was inaugu-
rated without blood.** 19 **For when every commandment
had been told to all the people by Moses in accordance with
the law, he took the blood of calves and goats, with water
and scarlet wool and hyssop, and sprinkled both the scroll
itself and all the people,** 20 **saying, "This is the blood of
the covenant that God has ordained for you."** 21 **And
in the same way he sprinkled with the blood both the tent
and all the vessels used in worship.** 22 **Indeed, under the**

**law almost everything is purified with blood, and without
the shedding of blood there is no forgiveness of sins.**
23 **Thus it was necessary for the sketches of the heavenly
things to be purified with these rites, but the heavenly things
themselves need better sacrifices than these.** 24 **For
Christ did not enter a sanctuary made by human hands,
a mere copy of the true one, but he entered into heaven
itself, now to appear in the presence of God on our behalf.**
25 **Nor was it to offer himself again and again, as the high
priest enters the Holy Place year after year with blood not
his own;** 26 **for then he would have had to suffer again
and again since the foundation of the world. But as it is, he
has appeared once for all at the end of the age to remove sin
by the sacrifice of himself.** 27 **And just as it is appointed
for mortals to die once, and after that the judgment,**
28 **so Christ, having been offered once to bear the sins of
many, will appear a second time, not to deal with sin, but to
save those who are eagerly waiting for him.**

CORE VERSE

He is the mediator of a new covenant, so that those who are called may receive the promised eternal inheritance.
(Hebrews 9:15)

OUR NEED

Once I found that I needed help in doing some remodeling on my house. I can do some minor carpentry work and painting; but when it comes to laying foundations, installing windows, or finishing dry wall, I am out of my depth. So I called a friend who had done some construction for me before and asked him to give me a bid. A few days later he brought me a detailed listing of the materials and labor he needed for the project along with the cost of doing the job. I agreed to pay him that amount of money if he would construct the building. We signed a contract, and a few days later the work began.

My friend agreed to do something for me, and I agreed to do something for him. Our agreement bound us to fulfill our promises, and either of us could be held liable by the courts if we failed to do our part. This kind of agreement may be called a contract, a bargain, a pact, or a treaty, depending on what is being agreed upon and who is doing the agreeing. All of them are covenants between two parties that are binding until the conditions are fulfilled.

God made such an agreement with his people at Mount Sinai when the commandments were given. This covenant, often called the law in the Bible, was the agreement between God and his chosen people. They were to observe his laws, and in return God would be with them in every circumstance of life.

That covenant had been in effect for many generations. A new covenant had been promised in the time of the prophets, but it had not yet been instituted. For Christians, the fulfillment is in the person of Jesus Christ. He has become the "guarantee" (Hebrews 7:22) of the better covenant.

FAITHFUL LIVING

The Letter to the Hebrews is well named. It obviously is addressed to persons who are quite familiar with the Jewish faith. The Gentile world would have known very little about such matters as the law and the prophets or the high priesthood or the covenant of God with the nation of Israel, but all these subjects were of great concern to the writer of Hebrews. He believed it was very important that Jesus Christ be understood clearly as the one who fulfilled the expectations of the law and the prophets as the Hebrew people understood them.

We already have seen how the writer of Hebrews dealt with the matter of the priesthood. In these passages we will see how he related the new covenant to the old.

The purpose of the original covenant was to establish the dependability of the God who brought the Hebrews out of Egypt and to outline the rules under which the people would live. (The books of Exodus, Leviticus, and Deuteronomy contain many of these rules.) The Christians needed to find a way to describe God's dependability for their own day. How would they go about it?

The writer of Hebrews appealed to history. He reviewed the experience of the chosen people and quoted from their Scriptures. He reminded his readers what the original covenant said. He recalled that a new covenant had been promised by quoting from Jeremiah 31:31: "The days are surely coming, says the LORD, when I will make a new covenant with the house of Israel." He believed that God was not changing the rules suddenly but was completing his promise.

The writer then appealed to reason. He pointed out that "if that first covenant had been faultless, there would have been no need to look for a second one" (Hebrews 8:7). Nothing was wrong with the old covenant as far as it went, but it did not go far enough. Now a new covenant had come that was far greater than the old.

The writer and his readers knew that history and reason must give way to the Word of God through his Son and those who followed him. The final act of God must go beyond the past and beyond what human beings can deduce from the past through rational process. God has revealed himself once more to his people in a way that is both tied to the past and separated from it. The new covenant is now the standard of God's relationship to his people. God has shown himself to be dependable again. It remains to be seen whether his people will keep their share of the covenant.

In what ways do you feel that you are observing your covenant with God?

Comparing the Covenants

To modern ears the extended discussion of the differences between the covenants may seem to be unnecessary. We have come to accept the process of salvation through the death of Jesus Christ so thoroughly that we do not even question its connection with the processes of the past. We either accept or reject Christ on his own merits rather than in terms of the history of Israel. But first-century readers of the Book of Hebrews needed the connection. Most of them were either followers of the Jewish faith or knew about it through association with the synagogues and communities of faith. It may help us as well to review that relationship.

In the previous chapter we discussed the change from legalism to grace. Throughout Hebrews the writer constantly reminds us that we no longer are under the threat of an angry God. We always are able to anticipate the compassion of One who cares for us enough to experience what it means to be human and to die on the cross for our sins. An outline of the specific ways in which the new covenant demonstrates that change is found in Hebrews 9.

- The ***place*** where the covenant is celebrated has changed. The first place was the Tabernacle (tent), which was the established place of worship during the wilderness experience following the Exodus. The new tent is far beyond human construction and is a part of a cosmic reality.
- The ***approach*** to God is different. Under the old covenant only the priests could go into the inner sanctum, and they could do so only once a year. The new covenant, on the other hand, permits each person access without the necessity for any human intermediary. Christ has become the High Priest who "entered once for all into the Holy Place" (Hebrews 9:12) and left it open for us.
- The ***offering*** is different. In the old covenant the compact was sealed with the blood of animals sacrificed on the altar. Each year the covenant was renewed by offerings of

food and drink made on behalf of the people by the priests. The new covenant is established with the one offering of the blood of Jesus Christ, which never has to be repeated. That offering is good for all time and works for all persons.

- The ***result*** is different. The old covenant was for the cleansing of the outer person, but the new covenant penetrates to the heart. Under the old agreement "gifts and sacrifices are offered that cannot perfect the conscience of the worshiper" (Hebrews 9:9). The new will "purify our conscience from dead works to worship the living God!" (9:14). The whole prospect has changed. Instead of a ritual repeated once a year, the covenant now promises constant interaction with God in both redemption from sin and the achievement of a life of discipleship.
- Christ will ***return***. The final difference between the old and the new covenants is that the new covenant has a future. The old covenant repeated the original acts year after year. The new covenant offers a marvelous freedom to approach God in many ways. In time, Christ will come again to complete the celebration.

The Second Coming sometimes has become controversial in the Christian community because persons disagree about its exact circumstances. The New Testament warns us not to engage in such speculations, but we do anyway. A good rule for preparing for the Second Coming might be that it ought to involve the same preparations as getting ready for a long life. Whether the Second Coming is today or a million years from today does not change the covenant God has made with us: "that those who are called may receive the promised eternal inheritance" (Hebrews 9:15).

In what way do these descriptions of the nature of the new covenant make it any clearer to you?

The Fulfillment

As with other New Testament writers, the writer of Hebrews was concerned with relating the former actions of God to the present age. Hebrews never suggests that God has changed, only that circumstances have changed and that God moves to meet the needs of the times. We cannot carry outdated relationships with God with us throughout the rest of history. Some previous actions were performed in anticipation of certain results. When they happened, or did not happen, God then took other action to ensure that his people would continue to discover salvation through him. Those former actions have been fulfilled and are no longer required. Paul mentioned circumcision and the eating of meat sacrificed to idols as two such regulations that had outlived their usefulness.

Fulfillment is a basic theme of the gospel. The following are important reasons:

- ***Continuity is important.*** While we ought not to carry "the bones of our ancestors" into battle, we should not forget them either. The old covenant was not a waste of time. The old plan fulfilled its purpose when the new one began. The same God works in all ages for all people, even if in different ways at different times.
- ***Basic foundations are important.*** When we remember the primary purpose of the old covenant, we see that it was realized in the life of Israel. That covenant was established to provide forgiveness for the sins of the people. The covenant was a clear and understandable arrangement within the context of the day in which it came into being. Law codes were springing up all over the world, sacrifices were a part of many religious rituals, and the nations were competing for the recognition of their gods. So the form of the old covenant made it possible for the people of Israel to learn about God's salvation in the context of familiar practices. It is important that a new faith not be a radical change for worshipers. It needs to have familiar

elements and to be stated in terms that the people can understand. In that sense also the old covenant was fulfilled. It did its work in providing a foundation on which to construct the new covenant.

- ***Progress is vital in the development of relationships with God.*** Here, too, the old covenant was fulfilled. It was centered in the nation because the concept of individual rights and personal liberties had not yet been introduced. The centuries before the birth of Jesus witnessed a great explosion of insight in these areas. The Greeks and the Romans developed philosophies and legal systems that created a new consciousness of the worth of individuals. Until that time it would have been difficult for anyone to understand the concept of personal salvation. National gods and religions were all the people had.

The Jewish faith fulfilled a need and made progress possible, for the new covenant that stressed that every person came before God as an individual could be built upon it. A state religion was no longer necessary. All human beings were eligible to become children of God through faith in Jesus Christ alone.

In what other ways does the new covenant fulfill the old covenant? Which ways are the most important to you?

Conclusion

We can see that the new covenant was not a radical change from the old. We observe connections and continuations in almost every part of it, as well as new departures. The old covenant was neither abandoned nor overturned; it was incorporated into the new. The use of the term *fulfilled* is completely justified because each of the parts is shown to be a completed segment of a total plan that included both the old and the new. The final fulfillment, of course, awaits the triumph of God at the end of the age, an event we all confidently await.

CLOSING PRAYER

O God, who spoke to Moses and inspired the prophets, live in us today that we may continue to perfect our understanding of your plan for us until it is completed. In Christ's name we pray. Amen.

5

Chapter Five

CONFIDENT FAITH

PURPOSE

To realize how a confident faith in God enables us to endure life's circumstances

BIBLE PASSAGE

Hebrews 10:23-25, 30-39

23 **Let us hold fast to the confession of our hope without**
wavering, for he who has promised is faithful. 24 **And let**
us consider how to provoke one another to love and good
deeds, 25 **not neglecting to meet together, as is the habit**
of some, but encouraging one another, and all the more as
you see the Day approaching. . . .

30 **For we know the one who said, "Vengeance is mine,**
I will repay." And again, "The Lord will judge his people."
31 **It is a fearful thing to fall into the hands of the living**
God.

32 **But recall those earlier days when, after you had been**
enlightened, you endured a hard struggle with sufferings,
33 **sometimes being publicly exposed to abuse and perse-**
cution, and sometimes being partners with those so treated.
34 **For you had compassion for those who were in prison,**
and you cheerfully accepted the plundering of your posses-

sions, knowing that you yourselves possessed something bet-
ter and more lasting. 35 Do not, therefore, abandon that
confidence of yours; it brings a great reward. 36 For you
need endurance, so that when you have done the will of
God, you may receive what was promised. 37 For yet
"in a very little while,
the one who is coming will
come and will not delay;
38 but my righteous one will live
by faith.
My soul takes no pleasure in
anyone who shrinks back."
39 But we are not among those who shrink back and so are
lost, but among those who have faith and so are saved.

Hebrews 11:1-3
1 Now faith is the assurance of things hoped for, the con-
viction of things not seen. 2 Indeed, by faith our ances-
tors received approval. 3 By faith we understand that the
worlds were prepared by the word of God, so that what is
seen was made from things that are not visible.

CORE VERSE

Let us hold fast to the confession of our hope without wavering, for he who has promised is faithful. (Hebrews 10:23)

OUR NEED

In introducing the first chapter of this study, we said that it is important to separate personal faith from self-righteousness. We always have had difficulty with that distinction. We still do.

Was it faith or self-righteousness that was responsible for the suicide of almost one thousand followers of Jim Jones in Guyana in 1978? for the willingness of persons to be thrown to the lions in Rome? for the burning of barns by a Christian group in Canada to protest efforts to make them obey the laws of the state? for the sufferings endured by the first Christian missionaries to Africa? for the refusal of a group of parents in Hawkins County, Tennessee, to permit their children to read textbooks that contained ideas they disagreed with? for the actions of Joan of Arc? Each of these persons claimed that what he or she did was the result of confident faith. Which actually were?

What do we mean by confident faith? How can we know that we have faith, not some stubborn resistance to the realities of our world? Where does faith end and obstinacy begin?

FAITHFUL LIVING

Persecution was fresh in the mind of the writer of Hebrews. He spoke of public abuse, personal affliction, and the plundering of property. The letter was written to persons who had experienced the wrath of either religious or government leaders because of their faith.

Hebrews also was written to persons who did not have a personal experience of the time when Jesus was on earth. They may have been living during those years, but it is clear that the writer assumed that they were unfamiliar with the events themselves. Although they had no doubt heard witnesses speak about Jesus (Hebrews 2:3), the letter gives no indication that either the readers or the writer had personally witnessed the events.

That lack of knowledge surely was part of the reason that the writer stressed faith so strongly and defined it the way he did. He spoke of faith in terms of endurance, confidence, and perseverance. A faith that holds firm against threats and danger would be valuable, especially in times of persecution. It is also clear that faith is even more important when people have had no physical experience of the ministry of Jesus.

Persons who have seen believe because they saw, but people who have not seen must have a stronger faith to make up for their lack of knowledge.

The writer also worried about persons drifting away from the faith (Hebrews 2:1) and urged them to "hope to the very end" (6:11). They were not to lose hope, which is the "anchor of the soul" (6:19), but were to exhort one another to fresh efforts on behalf of the faith. He expressed worry about church attendance with the warning "not neglecting to meet together, as is the habit of some" (10:25). The first burst of enthusiasm had passed, and persons were finding that discipleship was not as easy as they once thought.

How like our own time! One of the continuing proofs of the divine inspiration of Scripture is its relevance to each region and generation. It fits all persons and places. While Christians are not persecuted in our country (although some Christians tend to punish others who do not agree with them), persecution is still a factor in many nations. Our faith is tested in a multitude of ways, including situations that tempt us to be complacent and uninvolved. We, too, must live by faith and not by sight because the days of the physical presence of Jesus are in the distant past. Hebrews truly is a letter to the twenty-first century as much as it was to the first century. The call to confident faith is never out of date.

Name some ways in which our faith is tested. How many of these ways have you experienced?

Proper Faith

Many years ago I went to Great Britain as part of a program of the Board of Home Missions of The Methodist Church. Staying in the homes of church members and preaching in churches in Wales and England was a delightful experience. One of the highlights was a visit to Mrs. Wilson who, at ninety-seven, was still actively interested in everything her church did. When we entered her home, the pastor said, "Mrs. Wilson, I'd like for you to meet our visiting minister from America." Mrs. Wilson tartly replied, "Oh, what kind of minister is he?" The pastor, taken aback, said, "Why, he's a Methodist." With a great sigh of relief Mrs. Wilson said, "Ah, a *proper* minister!"

Just as we have proper ministers, we have proper faiths. Jesus dealt with that matter in the temptations when he reminded Satan that it is not proper for persons to exercise their faith in such a way as to benefit personally (turning stones to bread) or to put God to the test (throwing himself off the pinnacle of the Temple). Some faiths are blind, some faiths are misguided, and some faiths are directed toward the wrong object. The wrong kind of faith can be a liability instead of a virtue.

Some time ago I compiled a list of Seven Deadly Virtues. They are

- ***Truth,*** if it becomes a weapon against persons.
- ***Beauty,*** if it becomes pride.
- ***Love,*** if it becomes possessive.
- ***Loyalty,*** if it becomes blind trust.
- ***Tolerance,*** if it becomes indifference.
- ***Self-confidence,*** if it becomes arrogance.
- ***Faith,*** if it becomes self-righteousness.

In the verses printed in our Bible Passage and in the portion of the eleventh chapter of Hebrews not printed, the writer defined some characteristics that make up a proper and confident faith. We will examine a few of these characteristics in the following paragraphs.

How did you feel when your faith in something or someone was disappointed? What did you do?

Faith Is Assurance

One of the most widely held views of faith is that it is a form of belief, that it means the acceptance of some concept or doctrine. When the term is used in the New Testament, and especially in Hebrews, it means a great deal more than that, however. One author has described it this way: "It is the act by which one lays hold on God's proffered resources, becomes obedient to what God prescribes and, abandoning all self-interest and self-reliance, trusts God completely" (from *A Theological Word Book of the Bible,* edited by Alan Richardson [MacMillan, 1951]; page 75).

Confident faith is giving and receiving the assurance that God is in his heaven and all is right with the world. It is the conviction that the world was created by the word of God and that God's Word continues to bring salvation to those who will accept him. It bridges the gap between what we see and what we can only take on trust. It is resting in the promises of God, an idea we already have discussed at length in Chapter 2. Confident faith provides us with the patience and self-control to endure the constantly changing circumstances of the world because we know that a place where all things finally become unchanging and secure is waiting for us.

What is the difference between faith as belief and faith as assurance?

Confessing Hope and Faith

Confident faith will seek an expression. Hebrews 10:23 exhorts us to "hold fast to the confession of our hope," which means that we will be strengthened if we remember how we felt when we acknowledged out loud the value of Jesus Christ in our life.

We must not confuse this confession with the recounting of our sins that is a part of the process of salvation. That experience is necessary and valuable, too; but the word used here means to stand with or to affirm rather than to admit error. We also could call it *pro*fession. We make a profession of faith when we confess that Jesus is Lord.

Faith is strengthened when it is declared. Witness is not only for the purpose of helping others find faith; it also has the value of helping us make our own faith more confident. In this way we discover resources for personal endurance of life's circumstances.

Can you write a confession of faith now? Try it, then share it with someone else.

Stirring Up Love in Faith

In the Letter to the Philippians, Paul commented that some persons preach Christ out of goodwill, but others preach from envy and rivalry (1:15). A part of the requirement that God places on Christians is to affirm the faith through acts and words that make for peace. A confident faith does not speak from defiance or attack others who may have a different expression. Instead, it speaks for itself, leaving the judgment about the faith of others to God.

Confident faith simply does not require aggressiveness. "The Lord will judge his people" (Hebrews 10:30) implies that no one else has to. When we claim superiority or special insight just because of the particular form of belief we have, we do not honor the Lord. Instead, we falsely credit ourselves with wisdom that rightly belongs only to God. A truly confident faith professes itself without demands. It is content to express itself without requiring that others accept the exact experience it reports. Through a variety of witnesses and forms, many will come to Christ. When we limit the acceptable responses that others may make, we destroy the value of our own confession and decrease the possibility that others will find a compatible mode for their discovery of salvation through Jesus Christ.

We are called to "provoke one another to love and good deeds" (Hebrews 10:24). When we make our confession of hope and faith in order to show our own joy in the Lord and when we receive the professions of others with enthusiasm and goodwill, we will find ourselves constantly sharing a common goal: the practice of a discipleship that sees and responds to the needs of every person in ways that make for peace and goodwill. In this way we help one another endure life's circumstances by giving meaning to one another's tasks.

What helps or barriers to loving Christian relationships have you practiced recently?

Confident Faith and Fellowship

Verse 25 of Hebrews 10 assumes that some persons were habitually absent from regular meeting times. Even the early church had inactive members! The writer of Hebrews obviously felt that confident faith is built by regular church attendance. While church may mean a small group meeting in the back of a business place or under the streets in a cave, it is just as necessary for the spiritual growth of individuals as if it were highly organized and had the best staff in the community. Here and elsewhere in the New Testament, we gain the idea that Christians cannot be expected to grow to maturity alone. They do best in settings that promote fellowship and interaction.

Many claim to be away from church fellowship because they do not find there the kind of warmth and spiritual nurture that they need. The church needs to listen to such persons and to do all it can to correct any defects in its ministry, but ultimately the individual must make the effort to find the kind of fellowship that will assist Christian growth. If the present church does not seem to be the right one, then find another. If another in which fellowship is possible cannot be found, then maybe the problem is with the person rather than with the organization. The habit of being absent from regular fellowship does not provide the opportunity to build confident faith.

The fellowship aspect of faith helps us endure life's circumstances. Within the circle of people who make up the church are some persons whose faith will supplement our own in times of distress and will join with us in periods of celebration.

What are some ways the church can better serve persons who seldom attend any church activity?

CLOSING PRAYER

O God, our life is made possible because we trust you. Help us live in such a way that you can trust us to do your work. In the name of Jesus Christ our Lord, we pray. Amen.

6

Chapter Six

DISCIPLINED COMMITMENT

PURPOSE

To discover how disciplined commitment leads to joyful Christian living

BIBLE PASSAGE

Hebrews 12:1-13

**1 Therefore, since we are surrounded by so great a cloud
of witnesses, let us also lay aside every weight and the sin
that clings so closely, and let us run with perseverance the
race that is set before us, 2 looking to Jesus the pioneer
and perfecter of our faith, who for the sake of the joy that
was set before him endured the cross, disregarding its
shame, and has taken his seat at the right hand of the throne
of God.**

**3 Consider him who endured such hostility against him-
self from sinners, so that you may not grow weary or lose
heart. 4 In your struggle against sin you have not yet resisted
to the point of shedding your blood. 5 And you have for-
gotten the exhortation that addresses you as children—**

**"My child, do not regard lightly the
discipline of the Lord,
or lose heart when you are
punished by him;**

6 for the Lord disciplines those
whom he loves,
and chastises every child whom he
accepts."
7 Endure trials for the sake of discipline. God is treating
you as children; for what child is there whom a parent does
not discipline? 8 If you do not have that discipline in
which all children share, then you are illegitimate and not
his children. 9 Moreover, we had human parents to disci-
pline us, and we respected them. Should we not be even
more willing to be subject to the Father of spirits and live?
10 For they disciplined us for a short time as seemed best
to them, but he disciplines us for our good, in order that we
may share his holiness. 11 Now, discipline always seems
painful rather than pleasant at the time, but later it yields
the peaceful fruit of righteousness to those who have been
trained by it.

12 Therefore lift your drooping hands and strengthen
your weak knees, 13 and make straight paths for your
feet, so that what is lame may not be put out of joint, but
rather be healed.

CORE VERSES

Let us run with perseverance the race that is set before us, looking to Jesus the pioneer and perfecter of our faith.

(Hebrews 12:1-2)

OUR NEED

Because my parents roused me from sleep at 5:00 A.M. to help with the milking and because my whole family are physically "morning" people, I tend to rise early. Some people have the opinion that anybody who gets up early must be highly disciplined and very productive. I am living proof that that opinion is not correct. My early mornings often are spent cuddling the cat or watching the early news on television or reading the book I started the previous evening. When I remember that John Wesley prayed for an hour and studied for two more before dawn, I am often embarrassed by my morning sloth.

Of course, my early rising does come in handy when I have a deadline to meet, although my editors know that I do not always make my deadlines either. The problem I have is that I tend to operate from desperation rather than from discipline.

The previous statement does not mean that I am never disciplined. I have managed long periods of concentration. Once every two or three years, I succeed in losing a few pounds that I pick up when I am not paying attention. I quit smoking years ago. Every time I accomplish something like that, it makes me feel terrific. I usually tell everybody I see. I find real satisfaction and pleasure in disciplined commitment, even if it lasts only for short bursts. How much greater the joy if the commitment is to the greatest discipline of all, life in Christ.

FAITHFUL LIVING

As we do with other New Testament letters, we may wonder about the people to whom Hebrews was written. Many of the New Testament letters have a salutation that identifies the recipient (See Romans 1:7; 1 Thessalonians 1:1; 2 Thessalonians 1:1.), but Hebrews does not. It contains no indication of either the sender or the receiver, except a brief reference in 13:24 to greetings from Italy. Only the title, which was placed on the letter sometime during the first century, gives a clue; and it is very little help. It could refer to a single group of people or to a whole region. We know a great deal about the people of Corinth and Philippi but almost nothing about the "Hebrews" who received this letter. Some clues, however, will allow us to speculate a bit.

As we have already said in another chapter, we know that the "Hebrews" were Christians who learned the faith from preachers and teachers rather than from Jesus or the apostles. The witnesses spoken of in Hebrews 12:1 are the same ones referred to in Chapter 11: Abraham, Moses, Barak, and the prophets, not those who were present when Jesus was alive.

We also know that the "Hebrews" had been persecuted in various ways but probably not recently. The memory was still alive, but enough time had passed that complacency had set in again. In other times and places persons were burned at the stake or thrown to the lions; but not there, wherever that was.

Since Rome was the place where major persecutions took place and since the reference to Italy in Hebrews 13:24 seems to imply greetings from that country, we assume that this letter was directed somewhere else, probably to Christians living in a city other than the ones referred to in the other letters.

We can assume that a large number of the letter's recipients were Jewish Christians because of the great concern with establishing a connection with the religious experience of the Jewish faith. But they probably lived outside the Holy Land because the quotations from the Old Testament are from the Greek translation, called the Septuagint, rather than from the Hebrew. For that reason, the quotations are sometimes different from the New Revised Standard Version and other English versions that are based on the Hebrew original rather than on the Greek.

The "Hebrews" were probably part of a church in a community somewhat separate from the mainstream but still active in the Christian movement. The community was important enough to be the recipient of a major letter from headquarters, but it did not have leaders who were so well known that they could be mentioned by name. In fact, this community may have had problems with leadership because the writer mentions that few teachers have emerged and that their view of the Christian life is still very elementary (Hebrews 5:12). It may have been a fairly large church but one that did not have an outstanding record.

In other words, here is a church without distinction but without grave faults either. It was an average church, much like our own. It had had some hard times in the past but was much more comfortable at present. It supported the mission movement but did not send anyone from its own ranks. It received letters but did not write them. It paid its part of the general church benevolences reluctantly but without rebellion. Whether it was a single church or the whole church of that region, it already was beginning to look like the church of today. It was exactly the kind of church that would benefit most from a letter about commitment and joyful Christian living.

After studying the Letter to the Hebrews, what can you add to the description of the people who received it?

The Call to Discipline

The writer of Hebrews developed the themes of the letter well. He made a statement of the resources of the faith and offered some interpretations that added to the overall understanding of the process of salvation through Jesus Christ. Then he came to the heart of the matter: What good is a statement of faith unless someone acts on it?

"Let us lay aside every weight" (Hebrews 12:1). Perhaps we can deduce the meaning of this sentence from a handicap horse race. The horses who are stronger or faster or who have lighter jockeys must have weights added to the saddle to even the odds. These impediments to full performance are for the benefit of the bettors, not the horses.

The weights make each one start from the same place. Hebrews says that that procedure is not good enough. We must give everything we have, which means that some people will be giving more than others because they have more to give.

Then we are commanded to "run with perseverance the race that is set before us" (Hebrews 12:1). The key word here is *perseverance.* It is not enough to start with a bang or even to come on strong at the end. A great Christian life is one in which the disciple keeps doggedly to the goals of the gospel in all stages of life and through all kinds of circumstances. It is a marathon race rather than a one-hundred-yard dash, and the prize goes to the one who keeps the pace most consistently rather than to the one who has the best style or who puts on the biggest burst of speed in front of the grandstand.

This form of discipline is even more difficult because it often robs us of the chance to take credit or to receive praise for some dramatic action. We are asked to be satisfied with the progress of the kingdom of God and not to worry about the state of our own public relations. That rule is not easy to obey in any race!

The call is reasonable, however, because we are "looking to Jesus the pioneer and perfecter of our faith" (Hebrews 12:2). A model has been provided. We can see how it is done. The very fact that Jesus lived a faultless life makes us more confident that we can live a spiritually successful life ourselves. When we had only the standards of the law for guidance, we never knew where we were; but since the "perfecter of our faith" has come, we have a new relationship with God. Discipline is more possible because we now know what is expected of us and what we can expect of God.

Furthermore, we are called to a discipline less than Jesus endured for us. Like us, the readers of Hebrews had not been called upon to shed their blood for their faith. While others have been in the past and we might be in the future, the majority of us will be asked to give something less than our physical lives. That knowledge may be a great advantage, but sometimes it is misleading. We admire the people who gave everything for the faith, but we sometimes balk at giving up small luxuries. Still, everyday discipline does the most for the Kingdom. "Do not regard lightly the discipline of the Lord" (Hebrews 12:5).

So we are called to live disciplined lives. The next question we might ask is, What do we get out of it? We will look at answers to that question in a moment.

In what ways, and by whom, have you been called to discipline? Do you think any of these has been the voice of God? What have you done in response?

The Values of Commitment

Disciplined commitment has a number of valuable effects on people who practice it. The first of these effects is pointed out in Hebrews 12:10: "He disciplines us for our good, in order that we may share his holiness." Discipline builds character.

We must quickly distinguish between discipline and punishment. The difference is in the objective. Punishment is given for errors made, in order to correct our behavior. Discipline prepares us for a more productive experience. We keep a regimen of diet (discipline) in order to look and feel better. We develop a savings plan and keep it (discipline) so that we can afford to buy a car or a new home or some needed item. We have a planned time for study and prayer (discipline) because we want to know more about the spiritual life. These disciplines not only help us reach our immediate goal; as we practice them, these disciplines create a reservoir of strength that can serve as the foundation for other efforts. This foundation is called "character" when it involves the building of positive images of ourselves in relation to God and the public good.

Discipline also gives us self-assurance. It is amazing to discover that even people who are shy and self-effacing will develop confidence in themselves when they learn a new skill or prove that they can achieve a difficult goal. The Special Olympics helps us rediscover each year that persons who discipline themselves to any task feel better about themselves in every area of their lives.

Discipline enables us to be creative. While the repetitive routines of the disciplined life may seem to be just the opposite of the freedom of creativity, it turns out that they are closely tied to one another. The acrobat who flies through the air with the greatest of ease is able to soar because he or she has spent many hours of practice on the basic skills of the craft. Acrobats learn their craft so well that they no longer have to think about each action.

The writer of Hebrews reminds us that we too must "go on toward perfection, leaving behind the basic teaching about Christ, and not laying again the foundation: repentance from dead works" (6:1). Of course, we are warned in other places that it takes a lot of time to develop the fundamentals; but a time comes when creativity in the faith is possible if we have done our homework.

Discipline frees us to be our best self. Before my retirement, I went to a lot of meetings as a spectator but more often as the person responsible for arranging the setting, making the agenda, and providing information and resources. When I had made myself get ready and felt that I had prepared all the necessary ingredients, I could be very genial; but when disciplined preparation was lacking, I was often distracted, worried, and gruff. I was a happier person because of the discipline of preparation.

In the same way, the joy of the Christian life is greater when we have developed the ability to be our best spiritual self through a consistent practice of the elementary ingredients of the spiritual life: prayer, study, stewardship, and holiness. On these elements can be built the winsome disposition and radiant face of the true disciple.

Disciplined commitment leads to joyful Christian living, not because discipline is fun (although it may be), but because it develops character, self-assurance, and the possibility of creativity in order that we may become our best selves for Jesus Christ. We are called to that commitment not only in the study of this letter but also in the whole word of God through the Scriptures. We can do no less.

What disciplines are easy for you to practice? What joys do you find as a result?

CLOSING PRAYER

O God, you have called us to a life of practical spirituality. Provide us with the will to practice the basics so that we may discover the ecstasies of the faith. In Christ's name we pray. Amen.

7

Chapter Seven

DAILY CHRISTIAN LIVING

PURPOSE

To learn from the example of Jesus Christ how we can live as Christians in our time

BIBLE PASSAGE

Hebrews 13:1-16

**1 Let mutual love continue. 2 Do not neglect to show
hospitality to strangers, for by doing that some have enter-
tained angels without knowing it. 3 Remember those who
are in prison, as though you were in prison with them; those
who are being tortured, as though you yourselves were being
tortured. 4 Let marriage be held in honor by all, and let
the marriage bed be kept undefiled; for God will judge for-
nicators and adulterers. 5 Keep your lives free from the
love of money, and be content with what you have; for he
has said, "I will never leave you or forsake you." 6 So we
can say with confidence,**

"The Lord is my helper;
I will not be afraid.
What can anyone do to me?"

**7 Remember your leaders, those who spoke the word of
God to you; consider the outcome of their way of life, and**

**imitate their faith. 8 Jesus Christ is the same yesterday and
today and forever. 9 Do not be carried away by all kinds of
strange teachings; for it is well for the heart to be strength-
ened by grace, not by regulations about food, which have not
benefited those who observe them. 10 We have an altar
from which those who officiate in the tent have no right to
eat. 11 For the bodies of those animals whose blood is
brought into the sanctuary by the high priest as a sacrifice for
sin are burned outside the camp. 12 Therefore Jesus also
suffered outside the city gate in order to sanctify the people
by his own blood. 13 Let us then go to him outside the
camp and bear the abuse he endured. 14 For here we have
no lasting city, but we are looking for the city that is to come.
15 Through him, then, let us continually offer a sacrifice of
praise to God, that is, the fruit of lips that confess his name.
16 Do not neglect to do good and to share what you have, for
such sacrifices are pleasing to God.**

CORE VERSE

Do not neglect to do good and to share what you have, for such sacrifices are pleasing to God. (Hebrews 13:16)

OUR NEED

In another publication I write for, I mentioned that I was from Slant, Virginia. A reader contacted the editor to protest that there was no such place. When I sent the reader some photographs of the swinging bridge, the house where I was reared, and one of the few maps that listed the location by name, he wrote back to tell me about his childhood in a place just like Slant. For him, and for me, the days of our childhood were days to treasure.

In these nostalgic times we tend to admire rural values. Many of those who have "made it big" purchase farms and retreats far from the city in order to have a place of escape from the din of civilization. But for those of us who grew up in the places everybody wants to retreat to, it was not always a rosy situation. At times we thought that we were looked down on and felt unwelcome in the more sophisticated towns and cities. It was probably partly our own fault, but we had a sense of being "outside the camp."

We are now in the mainstream, however. It is hard to know whether that is a good thing. Perhaps we have mixed our values rather than purifying them. Some of the worst parts of "country" have intermingled with some of the bad parts of "city" to make a confusing combination. Possibly we are losing some of the best of both.

Has that situation also happened to the Christian faith? Christianity has a wide acceptance. We hear it proclaimed everywhere. The public media, the government, and celebrities are often outspoken in support of Christianity. But are those "outside the camp" receiving ministry, and is this popular version of Christianity the real thing?

FAITHFUL LIVING

The faith has always had some dramatic stories. The early church certainly had its share. Pentecost, the ministry and stoning of Stephen, the travels of Paul and other missionaries, and the martyrdom of persons who defied government and religious leaders in order to proclaim the faith are thrilling episodes. We all have heard these stories and tend to look on them as the story of the early church. But for the writer of Hebrews, the real story was the behavior of common people in ordinary circumstances.

That theme is true to the memory of Jesus, who taught constantly about the need to be in ministry wherever we are. He spoke of the good Samaritan, the talents, crusts of bread, and visits to prison. Hebrews strikes the same chords. The standards of Christian behavior are not measured in power or numbers but in the development of caring relationships within and outside the community of faith.

The Christian community is never considered superior or special by the writer of Hebrews. Only Jesus Christ is superior. The hallmark of the community is faithfulness to the vision of Jesus Christ. The claims of present-day Christian groups to some form of superiority because of a belief or practice are unacceptable in this view of the meaning of responsibility. Only obedience counts; and this obedience must be to the whole purpose of the act of salvation, not to some particle of it that suits the whims or personal aspirations of self-proclaimed religious leaders.

The call of Hebrews is to a personal Christian ministry, to a daily act of obedience to the vision of Jesus that we become as little children and love our neighbor as ourselves.

What are some evidences that persons choose power rather than ministry?

Examples of Faith Expression

It is significant that the list of daily responsibilities in our Bible Passage begins with "Let mutual love continue" (Hebrews 13:1). Nothing is so important as affection among members of the congregation of the faithful. The value placed on this characteristic by Paul, by the writer of the Letters of John, and by Jesus himself cannot be overestimated. Repeatedly we are reminded that it is more important to love one another than it is to agree with one another (Romans 14:1-4; Galatians 5) or even to have the right doctrine (Romans 15:1-5; 1 John 3:18). For the early Christian community, nothing was as important as the fellowship of believers. Whenever we have neglected to remember that fact, we have suffered losses and divisions in the body of Christ.

The second expectation is almost as pointed. "Do not neglect to show hospitality to strangers" (Hebrews 13:2). The same love that we are to extend to members of the household of faith must also be shared with those who are outside the faith.

Growing up in the country did have its good points. When we wanted to visit someone, we just dropped in. We did not wait for an invitation or make phone calls in advance. We just went on by. And people came by to see us. Sometimes they were people we did not know, strangers who wanted to talk to my dad about music or to get a good meal at my mother's table.

Those times probably are over. Not many strangers drop in for lunch these days. But that does not mean that the responsibility to be hospitable is over. Strangers everywhere need a sense of belonging, a kind word, a warm welcome. Neighborhoods, homes, and churches need to open their doors to strangers. I remember a stranger who wanted to worship on Easter Sunday in a friendly small town church who went away sadly because no one had spoken to him. The world is full of lonesome strangers whose only hope is Christian charity. Times have not changed that much. We could still be entertaining "angels without knowing it" (Hebrews 13:2).

"Those who are in prison" (Hebrews 13:3) implies a third level of care. We are responsible not only for the stranger in our home and community but also for those who have committed crimes. Some say that the writer meant to say that we should visit Christians who are in jail in order to witness to them, but such an interpretation would not be in keeping with the words of Jesus or with the letters of Paul.

In fact, we are responsible for those who are ill treated in any way, "since [we] also were in the body" (Hebrews 13:3, footnote *u*). It is only a guess, but it seems logical that the writer was reminding us that we are part of humankind also and that our need may one day be as great as the needs of those whom we help today. Some persons are mistreated because they are unlike us, some because we are rude or indifferent, and others because we are part of a society that expects us to show contempt for certain other people.

In *The Crucial Decade* (by Eric Goldman [Vintage Books,

1961]; page 183), a book about the 1950's, one of the stories illustrates our failures all too well. In the middle of the Korean War, the body of Sergeant John Rice was brought to Sioux City, Iowa, for burial. Officials of the Sioux City Memorial Park stopped the ceremony because Sergeant Rice was a Winnebago Indian. Only members of the Caucasian race could be buried in that cemetery. The honor of the nation was upheld when President Truman ordered an Air Force plane to fly the body to Arlington to be buried in the National Cemetery. Such incidents have been a part of every section of the country at some time.

A few years ago it was African Americans, and today it may be Asians or Spanish-speaking citizens or persons who have alternative lifestyles who are held up to ridicule, are made to feel inferior, or actually are abused physically. Whether the mistreatment is a result of a failure on the part of society or of the person who is being abused is not relevant. Christians are responsible for seeing that all those who are mistreated are protected from the prejudices and inhumanities of all persons everywhere, including our own.

The sanctity of marriage is also part of the expected response of Christians to the example of Jesus Christ (Hebrews 13:4). The idea of sexual repression is found nowhere in the New Testament, but a clear requirement of sexual fidelity in the marriage bond is present. Marriage is the only condition under which we can express sexuality freely, and we are to keep the vows of the bonds of matrimony under all circumstances. God is the judge of morality, however. It is not necessary for us to become arbiters of behavior for others. God will take care of that. It is our responsibility to care for our own morality and to leave to God the judgment of those who transgress his law.

"Keep your lives free from the love of money" warns the writer in Hebrews 13:5. As other parts of the New Testament, Hebrews clearly identifies the love of money as the root of evil. The drug trade, housing discrimination, crime, gambling, prostitution, and many other social and personal ills are the result of a desire for money. In our own sphere we may reflect that same failing in our efforts to feather our nests in minor ways. Sometimes even the best of us show an excessive interest in the accumulation of wealth. The desire for travel, fine homes, and comfortable lifestyles may be little different from organized crime if we expend our best efforts to attain them rather than seeking first the kingdom of God.

Finally, we are reminded to remember spiritual leaders, "those who spoke the word of God to you; consider the outcome of their way of life" (Hebrews 13:7), which warns us not to put ultimate faith in guides until they have proved themselves by living the kind of life that befits the gospel. Persons who labor in the Lord's field are to be held in high esteem and cared for by the Christian community, however. We are not certain that the early church had paid leaders as we do; but in every other way the Word is clear: Cherish those who witness to the faith.

Daily Christian living may not be glamorous, but it is critical. All of the above are vital ingredients of a living faith. While notoriety and visibility may be valuable in the arena of Christian leadership, the real measure of the faithful person is how well his or her life conforms to Jesus' example.

What other areas can you add to the list of Christian responsibilities in today's world?

The Ultimate Responsibility

A key line appears in Hebrews 13:14: "For here we have no lasting city, but we are looking for the city that is to come." As much as we may love and value the whole range of human experience, including the love of friends and the warmth of the church, this world is not our home. Instead, we are citizens of the household of God (Ephesians 2:19). Our ultimate responsibility is not to any human government or institution or agency but to the saving of the nations through Jesus Christ. Because of that responsibility, we are to be aware that the major arena for our ministry is "outside the camp" (Hebrew 13:13).

Whatever may be the exact meaning of that phrase, we can be sure that it calls us to daily Christian living in a universal dimension. Our responsibility has no cultural, geographical, or temporal limits. Those people outside the camp are more to be sought even than those within.

In my home place we sang songs that were not accepted as great music by some Methodist hymnists. I still smart a little when people criticize those songs. They were the faith to us. Many of us learned new songs in other places, but the old songs still tugged at our hearts. It is a tragedy when a choice of hymns puts someone outside the camp.

How much more of a tragedy it is if race, language, gender, political conviction, or physical appearance becomes a barrier to full acceptance. It is not possible for Christians to call themselves by the name of Jesus and support such barriers. We are required to strive with Christ for those outside the camp, that all may come to God through him. In the words of God through Paul, "All this is from God, who reconciled us to himself through Christ, and has given us the ministry of reconciliation" (2 Corinthians 5:18).

What must you do to bring reconciliation to those outside your circle? What must the church do?

CLOSING PRAYER

O God, you have made the earth and all that is within it. Give us the will to love all you have made and to be the agent of redemption and reconciliation to all persons everywhere. In Christ's name we pray. Amen.